Introduction

As special operations forces (SOF) transition out of a decade of conflict in Iraq and Afghanistan, the SOF community needs to refocus on implementing Foreign Internal Defense (FID) campaigns to support Theater Security Cooperation Plan (TSCP) events for the Department of Defense's (DOD's) effort in security sector reform (SSR). As the skills of combined arms maneuver atrophied for the conventional army, so has the core SOF mission of FID for security cooperation events due to the kinetic nature of these recent combat engagements.

The role of FID in TSCP operations is a whole of government (DOD, Department of State (DOS), US Agency for International Development (USAID)) approach to decrease insurgency, subversion, lawlessness, and terrorism. Through a successful and Joint, Interagency, Intergovernmental, and Military nested execution of these operations in a security cooperation campaign; intrastate, and regional conflict or war can be deterred or prevented. Also, with the DOD entering into an era of downsizing and fiscal constraints, the investment in these engagement operations can prevent the large investment for another protracted low intensity war. However, a special operations campaign, developed and managed by the theater special operations command (TSOC), needs to ensure that SOF is engaging with the right partner, with the right capacities, and in the right location.

Following the creation of SSR, there has been successful execution of special operations campaigns. The case of the Philippines (Operation Enduring Freedom-Philippines) is an example of a long-term engagement strategy presenting desired effects in SSR. This was accomplished through a campaign created and managed by US Special Operations Command-Pacific (USSOCPAC). The force provider (1st Special Forces Group (Airborne)) provided feedback (partner assessments and progress of campaign objectives) to the TSOC to make campaign adjustments as the operational environment changed. This type of long-term engagement model

1

can be applied in other host nation (HN) engagement operations, to produce similar results over time and prevent future wars.

Research Question

This study aims to answer the question: How can special operations campaign planning support DOD efforts in SSR? To support answering this question, three elements must be understood. The first is how theater special operational commands plan and execute special operations campaigns in support of the geographic combatant commanders (GCCs). Second, is the unique contributions special operations offer to the DOD efforts in SSR. Finally, is how the special operations initiatives described by US Special Operations Command (USSOCOM) campaigns supporting these efforts, as the US Army seeks to evolve from the recent conflicts to combat future global threats.

By answering these questions and applying these discoveries to a complex political, military and global operational environment, this study aims to achieve two things. First, it will highlight the importance of integrated Joint, Interagency, Intergovernmental, and Military and special operations campaign planning and execution for the DOD's efforts in SSR. Also, it will solidify the importance for special operations campaign planning in a resource-constrained environment, enabling a focused approach to future global engagement.

Research Methodology

This study will explore TSOC implementation of security cooperation campaigns in support of SSR through the qualitative analysis of two case studies. The first case will examine a USSOCPAC campaign (Operation Enduring Freedom-Philippines) in the Philippines (2002-present). The second case study will be on the US Special Operations Command-Africa (USSOCAF) engagement with Mali (2001-2013), ending in the suspension of DOD engagement with Mali. Through this analysis, this study will compare the long-term effects of the special operations campaign to the effects desired by the SSR. Initially, SSR is compared to the joint military missions of FID and Security Force Assistance (SFA), in support of internal defense and development (IDAD) plans. The nesting of these campaigns compared against regional or global USSOCOM campaigns and initiatives. The intent is to provide a model or good practices for TSOCs to employ for the creation and management of special operations campaigns through identifying the positive and negative affects of TSOCs during the implementation of theater security cooperation campaign plans.

The selected cases offer many variances to compare and contrast. The primary variances are duration of engagements, geographic areas, and Joint, Interagency, Intergovernmental, and Military unity of effort. The first variance is the duration and frequency of special operations engagement. In the case of Mali, engagement was episodic, with sometimes years between engagements with Malian security forces. While in the Philippines, the engagement was enduring, with an established tactical command (Joint Special Operations Task Force-Philippines (JSOTF-P)) to execute the campaign. The next variation was different geographic areas of responsibility. Being executed by different TSOCs in Africa and South East Asia, the different geographic areas of responsibility offer unique cultural impacts on the campaigns' implementation. This variation also explores the planning and execution of separate TSOCs, mitigating the confounding variable of only examining one TSOC. The final variance is the alignment of special operations effort with interagency and intergovernmental efforts supporting SSR in the country. In the case of Mali, the USAID and DOS effort was focused on the economic growth in southern Mali, while special operations efforts disproportionally trained and equipped Mali security forces in the north to execute counterterrorism missions. Whereas, in the Philippines, the DOS, USAID, and special operations effort was more synchronized and provided a balanced execution of FID operations.

The cases are analyzed and compared against each other by the threat, ends, ways, and means. Understanding the threat is important to the execution of FID, because a transnational terrorist threat compared to localized insurgency has different lines of effort to reach the identified ends. The ends, or objectives, for a foreign partnership can change over time, but the study will identify the special operations objectives to see if a change to these ends affected the successful application of FID. The ways, or how, each implemented engagement strategy is studied by extracting the lines of operation from the operation approach from each case. The means, or resources, applied in each case are vastly different. These special operations resources will be identified and assessed if they were applied to offer a balanced approach of FID in support of SSR. The result of analyzing and comparing these variables will be a recommendation of a model or good practices for TSOCs to employ for the creation and management of special operations campaigns.

Theoretical Framework

This study is supported by the application of three theories. First is deterrence theory, which is from the international relations field of study. Second, also from international relations, is organizational theory. The third is an emerging special operations theory about the application of special operations in peacetime to mitigate conflict and prevent crisis. The synthesis of these three theories establishes the theoretical framework for the importance of special operations campaign planning in support of DOD's effort in SSR. Also, the theories will frame an understanding of the arguments presented throughout the study.

The realist, or neorealist, belief that a nation must use all instruments of national power to preserve the interest and security of the nation, lays the foundation for deterrence theory.[1]

---

[1] Bruce Berkowitz, "Proliferation, Deterrence, and the Likelihood of Nuclear War," *The Journal of Conflict Resolution* 29, no. 1 (March 1985): 112.

Deterrence theory is defined as, "a theory to implement preventive policy or strategies designed to dissuade an adversary from doing what it otherwise would do."[2] The theory has evolved drastically over the decades since it was first introduced in the early years of the Cold War. The father of the theory is the renowned US military strategist Bernard Brodie.[3] First introducing a model for naval application in *Sea Power in the Machine Age* in 1941, Brodie adapted this to combat the nuclear threat offered by the Soviet Union.[4] In writing *The Absolute Weapon: Atomic Power and World Order* in 1946, Brodie laid down the fundamentals of nuclear deterrence strategy for the United States. This initial version of the theory, or "basic deterrence," was to deter the direct nuclear attack on strategic targets within the territory of the United States.[5] This provided the theoretical basis for the Herman Kahn US foreign policy strategy of containment during the Truman administration, which the United States enacted until the fall of the Soviet Union. Since the Cold War, deterrence theory has been the catalyst to combat the proliferation of weapons of mass destruction, primarily nuclear weapons. Though not focused on deterring weapons of mass destruction, SSR seeks to deter instability, inter- and intrastate, by strengthening HN capacity and institutions. The application of deterrence in this way is primarily indirect, but can be direct in nature during combat FID operations like Iraq and Afghanistan. By conducting special operation campaigns during SSR, SOF can deter the sources of instability and a crisis for large-scale military employment can be prevented.

---

[2] Charles Kegley and Shannon Blanton, *World Politics: Trend and Transformation* (Boston: Wadsworth, 2012), 84.

[3] Bernard Brodie, "The Anatomy of Deterrence," *World Politics* 11, no. 2 (January 1959): 173-175.

[4] Ibid.

[5] Ibid.

Focusing on deterrence theory as a preventative policy approach for SSR exposes a similar and supporting theory. Liberal institutionalism tenants establish the basis for this second predominant theory on security reform and deterrence, which is organizational theory.[6] Created by Scott Sagan in the 1994, organizational theory originally focused on the role of international organization in nonproliferation and enforcement of international laws.[7] A broader evolution of this theory highlights the importance on international cooperation to combat instability during SSR. This is immediately evident as SSR was originally a United Nations initiative and program. The United States then adopted this framework for their HN security reform strategy. Through this cooperation, the United Nations and United States are able to leverage each other's capabilities and resources in an aligned approach. Also, organizational theory supports the cooperation and integration of regional intergovernmental organizations (like the European Union and Association of Southeast Asian Nations) during the application of SSR.

The emerging theory about the application of special operations in peacetime to mitigate conflict and prevent crisis was developed by Brian S. Petit (Colonel, US Army), while at the School of Advanced Military Studies. The concept is introduced in his monograph "Breaking Through the Tension: The Operational Art of Special Operations in Phase Zero."[8] This theory was further developed in the book authored by Colonel Petit, *Going Big by Going Small: The Application of Operational Art by Special Operations in Phase Zero.*[9] Identifying delineation between the Joint Operational Planning Process phases, Colonel Petit highlights the importance

---

[6] Scott D. Sagan, "The Perils of Proliferation: Organization Theory, Deterrence Theory, and the Spread of Nuclear Weapons," *International Security* 18, no. 4 (Spring 1994): 67.

[7] Ibid.

[8] Brian S. Petit, "Breaking Through the Tension: The Operational Art of Special Operations in Phase Zero" (monograph, School of Advanced Military Studies, U.S. Army Command and General Staff College, Fort Leavenworth, KS, May 2013), 1-4.

[9] Brian S. Petit, *Going Big by Getting Small* (Denver, CO: Outskirts Press, 2013), 1-11.

of Phase 0 (Shaping).[10] The slang descriptor know as Phase Zero, focuses the reader of his study on the pre-conflict engagement and SSR operations during this phase, which prevent the need to initiate Joint Operational Planning Process contingency (wartime) plans.[11] Through the analysis of historical special operations HN engagement in Yemen, Indonesia, Thailand, and Colombia, the scalable application of SOF during Phase Zero "sustains an advantageous peace, mitigates conflict, and prevents crisis or possibly war."[12] This theory identifies the utility of small-scale engagement through special operations campaigns to deter conflict. The synthesis of deterrence theory, organizational theory, and this SOF engagement theory provide the theoretical support for the special operations campaign support to SSR.

Background

This section provides the framework for what SSR is and how DOD efforts support the objectives. It compares SSR to the joint military missions of FID and SFA. This comparison will demonstrate how similar the missions of SSR and FID are through their execution, agencies, and objectives. It describes the relationship to the FID and IDAD and how they link to SSR. Finally, the FID execution and planning imperatives are described and analyzed against special operations efforts to support them. The objective of this section is to provide the background and understanding of SSR, to bridge further in depth analysis of special operation initiatives, missions, and campaign development later in the study.

---

[10] Joint Chiefs of Staff, Joint Publication 5-0, *Joint Operation Planning* (Washington, DC: US Government Printing Office, August 2011), III-38-III-39.

[11] Petit, *Going Big by Getting Small,* 53-56.

[12] Ibid., 2-3.

Security Sector Reform

Many US national and defense guidance documents reflect the strategic importance of SSR. In the *National Security Strategy*, all the initiatives to advance our national interests outlined by President Obama hinge on the synchronized application of the instruments of national power and engagement with partner nations.[13] SSR is a major component of this engagement. The objectives promote security and deter conflict through strengthened and expanded alliances and partnerships as outlined in the *National Defense Strategy*, and are dependent on the DOD activities conducted to support SSR.[14] The second pillar of the strategic framework outlined in the *Quadrennial Defense Review* supports these ideals through building security globally to preserve regional stability, and support allies and partners.[15] The common thread throughout these documents is that US national security is dependent on the ability to strengthen our allies and partners.

The origins of SSR began in the late 1990s as an approach to create stability through improved governance, development, and security.[16] Though largely an international concept, the United States adopted the program to "reform efforts directed at the institutions, processes, and forces that provide security and promote rule of law."[17] The objective of SSR is to assist partner

---

[13] US President, *National Security Strategy* (Washington, DC: The White House, May 2010). The 2010 NSS continues to highlight "engagement" as the primary mechanism for national security.

[14] Department of Defense, *National Defense Strategy* (Washington, DC: US Government Printing Office, June 2008), 9-11, 15.

[15] Department of Defense, *Quadrennial Defense Review* (Washington, DC: US Government Printing Office, March 2014), V.

[16] US Department of State, "Security Sector Reform," February 2009, accessed February 25, 2014, www.state.gov/documents/organization/115810.pdf, 1.

[17] Ibid.

governments to provide legitimate and accountable security to their populous, allowing these governments to then respond to internal and external threats to stability.[18]

The DOS, DOD, and USAID are the executing agencies for SSR.[19] The importance of the implementation of SSR have changed over the last decade as the conflicts in Iraq and Afghanistan bolstered increased interdependency and interoperability between these three agencies to reach their objectives. Documents, like National Security Presidential Directive-44, formalized the interagency partnerships to ensure that efforts were coordinated and not redundant or counter to each other.[20] This marked a formalized evolution from the previous US allied and partner security and development programs of the past.

The balanced approach to impact the HN systems not only focus on building professional security forces, but also seeks to reach these other SSR objectives: "establishment of relevant legal and policy frameworks; improvement of civilian management, leadership, oversight, planning, and budgeting capabilities; enhancement of coordination and cooperation among security-related and civil institutions; and management of the legacies and source of past or present conflict or insecurity."[21] Though SSR operations can focus on multiple objectives, the DOD's efforts largely target the last two objectives described above, with a primary role of "supporting the reform, restructuring, or re-establishment of the armed forces and the defense sector across the operational spectrum."[22]

---

[18] US Department of State, "Security Sector Reform."

[19] Ibid.

[20] US President, National Security Presidential Directive-44, "Management of Interagency Efforts Concerning Reconstruction and Stabilization" (Washington, DC: The White House, December 7, 2005), accessed October 15, 2014, http://www.irisc.net/site/Library/nspd-44.pdf, 2.

[21] US Department of State, "Security Sector Reform," 1.

[22] Ibid.

Foreign Internal Defense and Internal Defense and Development

Prior to SSR, the United States partnered with foreign nations to promote democracy, good governance with transparency and accountability, and human security.[23] For the DOD, these efforts focused on supporting the HN's IDAD plan. Joint Publication 3-22, *Foreign Internal Defense,* defines IDAD plans as the full range and measures taken by a nation to promote its growth and protect it from security treats.[24] To achieve the efforts outlined in IDAD plans, coordination is conducted between the HN and US agencies (primarily DOS and USAID). This coordination creates a balance of political, social, and economic development to combat instability. The DOD missions that support the IDAD are FID and SFA.[25]

FID is the "whole of government" approach, conducted by civilian and military agencies to enact programs with another government to protect the government and populace by preventing subversion, lawlessness, insurgency, and terrorism.[26] SFA concentrates on the DOD's effort in unified action. It not only develops foreign security forces to not only defend against the threats of subversion, lawlessness, insurgency, and terrorism, but also develops foreign security forces to defend against external state or regional threats. The extra external threat focus then builds their capacity to perform as part of an international coalition.[27] Though FID and SFA seem to be similar mission sets, they are not subsets of each other because SFA activities serve other

---

[23] Herbert Wulf, *Security Sector Reform in Developing and Transitional Countries* (Germany: Research Center for Constructive Conflict Management, 2004), accessed October 15, 2014, http://wulf-herbert.de/Berghofdialogue2.pdf, 3.

[24] Joint Chiefs of Staff, Joint Publication (JP) 3-22, *Foreign Internal Defense* (Washington, DC: US Government Printing Office, July 2010), xi.

[25] Ibid., I-16.

[26] Ibid., xi.

[27] Ibid., VI-31.

objectives beyond HN internal defense.[28] For this reason, the FID mission set will be the focus during this paper, as it encompasses a combined DOD, DOS, and USAID effort. Joint doctrine is expanding to designate both SFA and FID as the missions that contribute to the DOD role in SSR initiatives.[29] Even with this update to the joint doctrine, the FID mission will be the primary mission reviewed in the study, as it focuses on the primary special operations mission to expanding HN internal stability.

The National Security Council provides the initial objectives pertaining to the execution of FID, and the DOS is the lead government agency to help build and carry out the national FID policies and objectives.[30] USAID executes nonmilitary assistance programs focused on increasing development and domestic quality of life.[31] Under this construct, the DOD's execution of FID is the primary contribution to SSR, as it meets the DOD requirements established in SSR. The Office of the Secretary of Defense and the Joint Staff are the DOD national organizations that manage FID operations, which provide direction, authority, and policy for FID matters.[32] GCCs are then responsible for the planning and execution of FID operations within their prescribed area of responsibilities (AOR).[33] In certain cases the Secretary of Defense can authorize, through the Chairman of the Joint Chiefs of Staff, subordinate unified commands to conduct operations in support of FID.[34] Of specific importance are TSOCs because of the vital role of special

---

[28] Joint Chiefs of Staff, Joint Publication Note 1-13, *Security Force Assistance* (Washington, DC: US Government Printing Office, April 2013), viii.

[29] Ibid.

[30] Joint Chiefs of Staff, JP 3-22, xiii.

[31] Ibid.

[32] Ibid., xiii-xiv.

[33] Ibid., xiv.

[34] Ibid., xv.

operations in FID operations.[35] These authorizations will be important to remember later in this study, as the role of TSOCs in the case studies are reviewed in detail.

Foreign Internal Defense Imperatives

The imperatives for executing and planning FID operations are: to maintain HN sovereignty, understand long-term or strategic implications and sustainability of all US assistance forces, tailor military support to FID for the operational environment and the specific needs of the supported HN, ensure unity of effort and purpose, understand US foreign policy, understand the information environment, and sustain the effort.[36] These imperatives ensure that FID efforts do not boost instability or create the threats that FID is designed to combat. By analyzing the special operations role in each of the FID imperatives, the importance of a special operations campaign will become evident.

Through attentive special operations application of FID to support the IDAD, which is created by the HN, the HNs sovereignty is upheld. By understanding, the long-term or strategic implications and sustainability of U.S. engagement is vital to implementing a special operations campaign. This understanding is enabled through cultural training and enduring engagement with regionally aligned special operations force providers. Without this understanding, an unbalanced foreign security forces capability can be created, which can cause internal (military coup) or regional (interstate aggression) instability. Special operations offer the scalable capacity and capability options needed by DOD to tailor support to FID missions.[37] This allows flexible use of

---

[35] Joint Chiefs of Staff, JP 3-22, xv.

[36] Ibid., xvi-xvii.

[37] Capacity refers to a unit size and strength, where capability refers to the planning and operational training skills offered by special operations.

FID efforts as the US domestic, political, HN, and international operational environment interact and change over time.

Special operations, and specifically civil affair units, ensure the unity of effort and purpose by integrating not only all instruments of national power to support FID operations, but also coordinate intergovernmental and nongovernmental efforts as well. This is accomplished through a synchronized effort between the TSOC and HN DOS representation (embassy or consulate). Not only do special operation campaigns seek to understand the information environment during FID operations, but also they attempt to influence it through military information support operations. This gives the United States the ability to address regional, transregional, or global audiences during the execution of FID operations.[38] Finally, the SOF imperative of ensuring long-term sustainment meets the requirement to sustain the effort in FID operations.[39] This requires that all special operations in support of FID are "durable, consistent, and sustainable" by the HN.[40]

Special Operations

After providing the background to SSR, this section will further develop special operation's role within DOD's effort to SSR. First, to provide an overview of special operations the study will define what special operations are, who composes the organizations of special operations forces, and the command structure. Then special operations initiatives, campaigns, and missions will be analyzed and compared to their support to SSR. This will provide some of the ways and means that special operations use and employ during the conduct of SSR. The objective

---

[38] Joint Chiefs of Staff, JP 3-22, xvii.

[39] Headquarters, Department of the Army, Army Doctrine Reference Publication 3-05, *Special Operations* (Washington, DC: US Government Printing Office, August 2012), 1-15.

[40] Ibid.

of this section is to provide an expanded understanding of SOF initiatives and campaigns to the

DOD's support to SSR. This holistic understanding of the special operation role in SSR will

provide the foundation for the qualitative case study analysis in the following sections.

<u>Special Operations and Special Operations Forces Defined</u>

Understating an overview of special operations will continue to frame the provided

capabilities to the DOD's effort in SSR. Joint doctrine defines special operations as:

> Operations that require unique modes of employment, tactics, techniques, procedures, and equipment. They are often conducted in hostile, denied, or politically and/or diplomatically sensitive environments, and are characterized by one or more of the following: time-sensitivity, clandestine or covert nature, low visibility, work with or through indigenous forces, greater requirements for regional orientation and cultural expertise, and a higher degree of risk. Special operations provide the joint force commanders (JFCs) and chiefs of mission with discrete, precise, and scalable options that can be synchronized with activities of other interagency partners to achieve United States Government (USG) objectives.[41]

To highlight the advantages of employing special operations campaigns in SSR, this doctrinal

overview will be broken down and analyzed in pieces. First, the ability to employ special

operations in a range of environments, from permissive to denied or politically sensitive, offer

continued engagement with a HN, even during times of decreased security. Second, though the

majority of special operations in support of SSR are not characterized as time-sensitive,

clandestine, or covert, they are characterized as low-visibility, working through indigenous or

foreign security forces, cultural and regional alignment, and increased risk. These exhibited

characteristics offer politically palatable options for the United States to execute SSR. Finally, the

discrete, precise, and scalable options offered to the chief of mission or joint force commander

and synchronization with interagency partners, make SOF a key DOD asset during the execution

of SSR.

---

[41] Joint Chiefs of Staff, Joint Publication (JP) 3-05, *Special Operations* (Washington, DC: US Government Printing Office, July 2014), xi.

Special operations forces are "those active and reserve component forces of the Services designated by the Secretary of Defense (SecDef) and specially organized, trained, and equipped to conduct and support special operations."[42] SOF undergo a selection process, after which they receive specific training to attain expertise in special operations skills.[43] These personnel tend to be more experienced and many maintain proficiency in multiple military specialties (language, specialized insertion, etc.). SOF is inherently joint because the personnel and organizations come from different services. However, it is also joint and interagency coordinated because of the essential relationships required for special operations.[44] This joint and interagency relationship will be developed further during the discussion of SOF initiatives and campaigns. These attributes of SOF personnel provide a tailored force for the execution of special operations engagement campaigns in support of SSR.

Special Operations Forces Command and Control

The complicated special operations command and control is due to the joint nature of SOF and the specific mission leads that USSOCOM is given. An understanding of this structure is needed for this study to know the command relationships between the Secretary of Defense, GCCs, USSOCOM, TSOCs, and service component commands. Under DOD, SOF are part of each of the four services. The SOF component commands for the services are US Army Special Operations Command for the Army, Naval Special Warfare Command for the Navy, US Air Force Special Operations Command for the Air Force, and US Marine Corps Forces Special Operations Command for the Marines.[45] Of mentioning, a sub-unified command of USSOCOM

---

[42] Joint Chiefs of Staff, JP 3-05, GL-11.

[43] Ibid., I-5.

[44] Ibid.

[45] Ibid., I-3-I-4.

is Joint Special Operations Command which is "a joint headquarters charged to study special operations requirements and techniques, ensure interoperability and equipment standardization, plan and conduct joint special operations exercises and training, and develop joint special operations tactics."[46] Though Joint Special Operations Command is a sub-unified command under USSOCOM, like the TSOCs, the study will strictly focus on the TSOC campaign plan in support of DOD's effort in SSR.

USSOCOM is a unified combatant command with servicelike functions of resourcing, training, equipping, and providing joint SOF to the GCCs.[47] The four SOF component commands (US Army Special Operations Command, Naval Special Warfare Command, US Air Force Special Operations Command, and US Marine Corps Forces Special Operations Command) are designated by USSOCOM to provide manned, trained, and equipped SOF within their given services. Though not designated to a specific AOR like the GCCs, USSOCOM is the DOD's counterterrorism global synchronizer.[48] Under this global campaign plan, USSOCOM is a supported command for activities in combating global terrorism (formally known as the "global war on terrorism").[49] This gives operational control of SOF globally to the commander of USSOCOM in support of this global campaign plan.

The major subordinate unified commands of USSOCOM are the theater special operations commands, which "perform broad, continuous missions uniquely suited to SOF

---

[46] Joint Special Operations University, *Special Operations Forces Reference Manual, Third Edition* (MacDill Air Force Base, FL: Joint Special Operations University Press, 2011), 2-10.

[47] Joint Chiefs of Staff, JP 3-05, I-3.

[48] Ibid., II-7.

[49] Ibid., II-7-II-8.

capabilities."[50] Though a subordinate command of USSOCOM, the Secretary of Defense assigned operational control of the TSOCs and SOF units to their respective GCCs by way of the Global Force Management Implementations Guidance.[51] The TSOCs are Special Operations Command Europe, USSOCAF, Special Operations Command Central, USSOCPAC, Special Operations Command South, Special Operations Command North, and Special Operations Command Korea (who is under the operational control of US Pacific Command and delegated under US Force Korea).[52] The four service component commands provide the TSOCs with the SOF tactical units to execute the SOF missions within their respective GCCs AOR. The two primary TSOCs analyzed in this study are USSOCPAC and USSOCAF. The command relationship between the TSOCs, GCC, USSOCOM, and deployed SOF units is important to understand, because of how the SOF campaigns are executed in each of the case studies.

<u>Special Operations Forces Initiatives, Campaigns, and Missions</u>

The US joint doctrine is currently constructed around the defining of, and operating within, the operational environment, consisting of the physical domains of air, land, sea, and space; and the information domain of cyber.[53] Each of the physical domains is primarily dominated by a DOD service (Army is land, Air force is air and space, Navy is sea). During joint operations, the services combine their efforts under unified action across these physical and cyber domains. An initiative to explore the joint application of military power by the Army, Marine Corp, and USSOCOM identified that this occurred at the convergence of the land, cyber, and

---

[50] Joint Chiefs of Staff, JP 3-05, I-3.

[51] Ibid.

[52] Ibid.

[53] Joint Chiefs of Staff, Joint Publication 3-0, *Joint Operations* (Washington, DC: US Government Printing Office, August 2011), xv-xvi.

"human domains."[54] Known as Strategic Landpower, this joint commission of senior leaders identified the central, essential role of concept is to understand, influence, or exercise control within the "human domain."[55] The "human domain" is defined as "the totality of the physical, cultural, and social environments that influence human behavior in a population-centric conflict."[56] This parallels the populace or human centric approach of all efforts executed in SSR. As the Army and Marine Corps seek to update and integrate this domain into their doctrine, USSOCOM has begun by releasing *SOCOM 2020.*

Presented as a vision document for the future of US special operations, *SOCOM 2020* established four primary lines of operations: win our current fights, expand our global SOF network, preserve our force and families, and provide responsive resourcing. Attempting to create a paradigm shift within special operations, USSOCOM is seeking to rebalance SOF to embrace indirect operations in the "human domain" from using the current paradigm of direct operations to pursue terrorists wherever they are.[57] This initiative is rooted in the establishment and expansion of the global SOF network (GSN). The objective of the GSN is to "prevent or deter hostilities before they turn in major regional conflicts."[58] The concept of this network is to establish strong relationships between SOF and their foreign counterparts, and then employ US

---

[54] Raymond T. Odierno, James F. Amos, and William H. McRaven, White Paper, *Strategic Landpower: Winning the Class of Wills,* The Official Homepage of the US Army Training and Doctrine Command, October 2013, accessed October 15, 2014, http://www.tradoc.army.mil/FrontPageContent/Docs/Strategic%20Landpower%20White%20Paper.pdf, 2.

[55] Ibid., 4.

[56] US Special Operations Command (USSOCOM), *SOCOM 2020* (Tampa, FL: USSOCOM, May 2013), accessed October 15, 2014, http://www.defenseinnovationmarketplace.mil/resources/SOCOM2020Strategy.pdf USSOCOM, 1.

[57] Ibid.

[58] Ibid., 5.

expertise to expand capacity and capabilities of international SOF partners.[59] To increase the

capacity of the GSN, TSOCs will receive increased capabilities to bolster SOF support to their

respective GCCs.[60] Also, the network will be linked in more with interagency partners by

enhancing USSOCOM presence in the national capital region. These initiatives being executed to

expand the GSN can offer the transitional state needed to strengthen special operations campaign

support to the DOD's effort in SSR. This understanding of the SOF initiatives in the human

domain and GSN will provide needed context in this research during the analysis of the TSOCs in

the case studies and opportunities they offer to change during recommendations.

More of a vision statement than an operational framework, the ideals of *SOCOM 2020*

were used to create the SOF Operating Concept to provide strategies and innovations for special

operations in the future.[61] This concept provides opportunities for special operations to increase

their support to SSR, which are outlined in the key tenants of the concept. The first tenant,

expanding from the GSN, is "network building and sustained enduring relationships and

partnerships."[62] Another tenant of "enduring versus episodic engagement" supports partnership

building.[63] These tenants provide a sustained SOF presence to build the relationships and partner

capacity in HNs. The importance of these tenants will be expanded upon in the case study

analysis and recommendations later in the study. The central idea to these tenants is "you can't

---

[59]John D. Gresham, "SOCOM: Finding Certainty in Uncertain Times," *The Year in Special Operations 2014-2015 Edition* (June 2014): 22-23.

[60] USSOCOM, *SOCOM 2020,* 5.

[61] USSOCOM, *Special Operations Forces Operating Concept* (Tampa, FL: USSOCOM, May 2013), accessed October 15, 2014, http://fortunascorner.files.wordpress.com/2013/05/final-low-res-sof-operating-concept-may-2013.pdf, ii.

[62] Ibid., 4-9.

[63] Ibid.

surge trust."[64] Trust must be built over time before a crisis occurs, so the "institutions, mechanisms, and personal relationships" necessary to understand the operational environment and attain desired ends are established when a crisis occurs.[65] The final key tenant is "deliberate theater-level operations liking engagement activities and operational missions in time, space, and purpose."[66] This designates that TSOCs will conduct operational art and design to create engagement campaigns in the future. The coupling of these three tenants provide increased special operations support and opportunities to SSR.

The vision, strategies and innovations provided in *SOCOM 2020* and the SOF Operating Concept provide the framework for future SOF growth and evolution, but not a doctrinal campaign. The principal campaign that TSOCs are in support of is the Theater Campaign Plan, which is planned by their respective GCC. Other than direction on GCC AOR initiatives and guidance, the Theater Campaign Plan provides the TSOC with the "steady state authorities and funding that are typically associated with DOD security cooperation programs."[67] The security cooperation program that the majority of SOF FID operations are conducted in support of DOD's effort in SSR is the TSCP program. Initially referred to as the Theater Engagement Plan, the TSCP is "primarily a strategic planning document to link commander-in-chief planned regional engagement activities with national security objectives."[68] Within the TSCP program, the main method for SOF to conduct FID and SFA is under the Joint Combined Exchange Training (JCET)

---

[64] USSOCOM, *Special Operations Forces Operating Concept*, 6.

[65] Ibid.

[66] Ibid., ii.

[67] Department of Defense, *Theater Campaign Planning: Planners' Handbook* (Washington, DC: US Government Printing Office, February 2012), 5.

[68] Joint Chiefs of Staff, Chairman of the Joint Chiefs of Staff Manual 3113.01A, *Theater Engagement Planning* (Washington, DC: US Government Printing Office, May 2000), A-1.

program.[69] The JCET is a SOF specific pathway of engagement, where US SOF forces train side by side with a partner nation's security force.[70] The FID operations conducted in support of the JCET program are the focus of the SOF tactical engagement analyzed in each of the case studies. Understanding the linkages between the TCP to the JCET program provides the framework for later recommendations in the study, enabling the TSOC to plan and execute special operations campaign plans in support of DOD's effort in SSR.

Mali

On March 21, 2012, following the disintegration of Mali military forces and the coup by junior Malian military officers, the United States suspended military engagement with Mali.[71] At the time these events occurred in Mali, a popular political science narrative was that the special operations engagement with Mali troops had failed or possibly bolstered this instability.[72] Through this study, a deeper examination presents a different narrative of how special operation efforts changed over time for the better. The primary engagement factors that supported the engagement in Mali were the selection of the right Mali partner unit, special operation command focus, and episodic engagement. By exploring these factors, this Mali case study offers TSOCs

---

[69] Thomas K. Livingston, Congressional Research Service Report for Congress R41817, *Building the Capacity of Partner States Through Security Force Assistance,* Federation of American Scientists, May 2011, accessed October 15, 2014, http://fas.org/sgp/crs/natsec/ R41817.pdf, 37.

[70] Ibid.

[71] John T. Bennett, "Pentagon: All U.S. Elite Commandos in Mali 'Accounted For'," *U.S. News,* March 23, 2012, accessed June 17, 2014, http://www.usnews.com/news/blogs/dotmil/ 2012/03/23/pentagon-all-us-elite-commandos-in-mali-accounted-for.

[72] Peter Dorrie, "U.S. Special Operations Forces Screwed Up in Mali: Why Years of Military Cooperation Achieved So Little," The Medium, April 23, 2012, accessed June 17, 2014, http://www.medium.com/war-is-boring/u-s-special-operattions-forces-screwed-up-in-mali-643bc779751c.

some considerations and models to avoid and employ during planning and execution of special operations engagement campaigns.

Threat

To understand the threats (internal and external) to Mali's stability, the operational environment is briefly analyzed. Mali is a landlocked country in the northwestern panhandle of Africa. During decolonialization, Mali transitioned from a French colony to the democratic Mali Federation in 1960.[73] Like many former French colonies, the Mali Federation has transitioned between military and civilian rule over time. Though still independent today, French influences are still present in Mali, with French citizens and multinational corporations dispersed throughout the country. The northern portion of the country is in the Trans-Sahel belt that extends from west to east across ten countries and is dominated by the Saharan Desert. The populations in this desert environment are consolidated into small cities near water sources and some tribal nomadic groups that travel throughout the Trans Sahel and Sahara. These nomads travel freely throughout the Saharan Desert and rarely claim a state national identity. Southern Mali provides more arable land and contains about ninety percent of the country's population. Including the capital of Bamako, the south consolidates the majority of economic and political power in Mali.

The primary threat to Malian stability has been the tension between the northern populations and southern political authority, specifically the nomadic tribe known as the Tuareg. Inhabiting the northern region of Mali, this Berber tribe travels in the Saharan Desert, crossing the borders between Mali, Niger, Algeria, and Libya. The Tuaregs have rebelled three times in western Africa since 1916, in an attempt to establish sovereign Tuareg territories along their

---

[73] Central Intelligence Agency, "Mali," *The World Fact book,* June 20, 2014, accessed June 25, 2014, http://www.cia.gov/library/publications/the-world-factbook/geos/ml.html.

ancient migration routes.[74] The second rebellion, occurring in the 1990s, was an uprising against the Malian government because of the oppressive treatment of the Tuaregs by the military dictatorship in Bamako. Though transitioning from the military to civilian rule, the Malian government was perceived as excluding Tuaregs from political power. This rebellion was ended by the April 1992 National Pact between the Malian government and the Tuaregs.[75] This pact allowed for "integration of Tuareg combatants into the Malian armed forces, demilitarization of the north, economic integration of northern populations, and a more detailed special administration structure for the three northern regions."[76] The process of providing Tuareg autonomy was furthered by removing the structure of federal and regional governments in Mali and disseminating authority to the local levels.[77] These concessions should have created a lasting peace in Mali, but were broken by the spread of radical Islam in northern Africa beginning in 2001.

More of an insurgency than an offensive rebellion, the third rebellion (2006-present) is fueled by multiple factors. First, is the constant fight for complete Tuareg independence, not only in Mali, but across their ancestral lands. The second is the spread of radical Islam in northern Africa. The Libyan leader Mommar Gaddafi bolstered the spread of radical Islam in the Tuareg population. In the 1970s, Libya offered many economic opportunities to the Tuaregs and Gaddafi accepted them into the Libyan population. He also began training the Tuaregs as soldiers to

---

[74] Devon Douglas-Bowers, "The Crisis in Mali: A Historical Perspective on the Tuareg People," Global Research, February 1, 2013, accessed June 27, 2014, http://www.globalresearch.ca/the-crisis-in-mali-a-historical-perspective-on-the-tuareg-people/5321407.

[75] Ibid.

[76] Jennifer C. Seely, "A Political Analysis of Decentralization: Co Opting the Tuareg Threat in Mali," *The Journal of Modern African Studies* 39, no. 4 (2001): 510.

[77] Douglas-Bowers.

further his cause of Arab Nationalism in Africa, which was later exploited by radical Islam. The effects of this were seen in the second rebellion and throughout the spread of Islamic extremism in the Trans-Sahel, but were greatly increased in Mali following the overthrow of the Gaddafi led Libyan government in 2011. Without the protection of Gaddafi, the military trained Tuaregs returned home to their homes in northern Mali. The third factor is the influence of Al-Qaeda in northern Africa. In an effort to seek sanctuary from the war zones of Afghanistan and Iraq, Al-Qaeda in the Islamic Maghreb (AQIM) was establish in the Trans-Sahel to reconstitute and recruit for the transnational terrorist organization. Offering the Tuaregs economic opportunities and appealing with radical Islamic ideology, AQIM increased activities in northern Mali. This expanded the Malian threat from the desperate Tuareg factions, to the transnational threat of AQIM in the north.

Ends, Ways, and Means

With the primary threats to Malian stability being the third Tuareg rebellion and the spread of AQIM throughout those populations of the north; the ends (objectives), ways (how), and means (resources) that special operations engagement applied to these threats will be analyzed. As the global counterterrorism campaign synchronizer for the DOD, a primary objective for USSOCOM is to combat the spread and influence of AQIM in the Trans-Sahel region of northern Africa. Within Mali, these efforts target the operational strongholds in northern Mali. As a conduit to pursue this objective against AQIM, the FID efforts are aimed at building cooperation between the Malian government and Tuaregs and sustaining a Malian military opposition to AQIM in the north. These objectives in Mali were aided added by many US sponsored SSR initiatives, like: "Pan Sahel Initiative (PSI), Trans-Sahara Counterterrorism Partnership (TSCTP), African Contingency Operations and Training Assistance (ACOTA),

International Military Education and Training (IMET), Global Peace Operations Initiative (GPOI), JCETs, and Exercise Flintlock."[78]

The ways in which special operations engaged with Mali changed drastically over time. On a larger timeline, the United States began episodic engagement with Malian security forces following Malian independence. This engagement continued through the 1990s to 2001, but the episodic engagement (years between events) and random Malian military partnering did not provide increased gains to host capacity or enduring relationships to be created. Though supported by the increased spread of global terrorism following 9-11, special operation engagement in Mali did not increase until the United States identified the influence of AQIM in the region. In late 2006, Special Operations Command Europe established Joint Special Operations Task Force-Trans Sahara (JSOTF-TS).[79] This special operations command synchronized DOD's counterterrorism efforts in the region for European Command. The mission of JSOTF-TS is to "train, advise, assist, and equip partner nations and conduct other special operations as directed, in coordination with US Embassy country teams in the joint operations area."[80] The joint operations area was initially four countries but soon spread across ten countries in northwestern Africa and supported the DOD's efforts in SSR, outlined by the TSCT-P.[81] This expanded joint operations area required more of a regional focus of effort for JSOTF-TS, than a

---

[78] Simon J. Powelson, "Enduring Engagement Yes, Episodic Engagement No: Lessons For SOF From Mali" (masters thesis, Naval Postgraduate School, Monterey, CA, 2013), 2.

[79] JSOTF-TS was established by Special Operations Command Europe, because US Africa Command, and subsequently USSOCAF, was not establish and began initial operations until October 1, 2007.

[80] Joint Special Operations Task Force-Trans Sahara, "Mission," US Special Operations Command-Africa, accessed July 12, 2014, http://www.socafrica.mil/component/JSOTF-TS.asp.

[81] Max R. Blumenfeld, "Training in Trans-Sahara Africa," US Africa Command, December 13, 2010, accessed July 12, 2014, http://www.africom.mil/Newsroom/Article/7896/training-in-trans-sahara-africa.

country tailor approach that is needed in special operations campaign planning. Engagement did increase within Malian security forces, with the increase from two JCETs or JCET "type events" in FY08 to seven in FY09.[82] This shift was due to the increase in kidnappings for ransom of western hostages and targeted killings by AQIM in northern Mali.[83] Transitioning from episodic to enduring engagement, an assessment by USSOCAF highlighted some problems that JSOTF-TS had not forecasted with their special operations engagement campaign in Mali: the selection of the right Malian security force partner and the need for a Mali special operations liaison element.

The initial Malian security force partner selected for FID training through JCET events was the *Echelon Tactique Inter-Armee* (ETIA). The ETIA was selected because of the unit regional focus and locations that the unit had in Mali. Headquartered out of Gao, the ETIA units were tasked with providing defensive, and possible offensive, capabilities against instability in the northern districts of Mali.[84] These capabilities would protect the economic and political power in southern Mali, specifically Bamako. The systemic issues to partnering with the ETIA were not revealed until SOF started conducting JCETs with the ETIA units in 2009. A SOF officer who conducted JCET events with the ETIA from 10th Special Forces Group (Airborne) described the ETIA as:

> A company-sized, ethnically mixed, combined arms task force of approximately 160 men manned on a rotational basis – therefore not cohesive units. Basically motorized infantry formations, the ETIAs comprised infantry, armored reconnaissance, artillery, and support platoons/personnel.[85]

---

[82] Powelson, 7.

[83] Robert Fowler, *A Season in Hell: My 130 Days in the Sahara with Al Qaeda,* (Toronto: Harper Collins Publishers, 2011), 3-7.

[84] Powelson, 18.

[85] Ibid.

Every six months the soldiers of the ETIA would rotate back to their parent units across southern

Mali. The Malian military also considered a tour in northern Mali a hardship tour, similar to an

Afghanistan deployment for the US military. The entire northern Malian military forces would

rotate to the south every three years. So not only were the soldiers of the ETIA on a six-month

rotation, but the entire military was different in the north every three years. These Malian soldiers

were not only taking the training knowledge that might have been built with the last SOF

engagement, but also the DOS supplied military equipment that was distributed to the units. This

was illustrated during an engagement in December 2009, when a 10th Special Forces Group

(Airborne) Operational Detachment-Alpha facilitated the issuing of desert combat uniforms

(DCUs) to soldiers of ETIA 4.[86] By June 2010, more than half the formation was back to the

standard black combat uniform and zero desert combat uniforms were present a few months later,

thus demonstrating the high rotation of soldiers through the ETIA and equipment loss.[87] This

equipment problem, coupled with the rotational aspect of Malian soldiers in the ETIA and

northern Mali, underscored the larger issue of sustaining or building capabilities within the ETIA

to the SOF conducting the engagement.

These issues identified by the special operations force providers and USSOCAF led to an

adjustment in the special operations engagement campaign in Mali. The first change was an

increase in the duration and number of TSCP events with the ETIA. This was demonstrated by

the durations of events shifting from thirty to forty-five days, and then eventually to three months.

The number of JCET events increased as well, with two in 2008 to nine in 2009, and then

persistent six-month rotations in 2010.[88] The second change was the creation of a USSOCAF

---

[86] Powelson, 20.

[87] Ibid.

[88] Ibid., 28-29.

forward command in Mali, by forming a Special Operations Forces Liaison Element (SOFLE) and a Joint Planning Assistance Team (JPAT).[89] Though primarily manned by elements from special operations force providers, the SOFLE and JPAT gave SOCAF the command needed to plan and assess the special operations campaign in Mali. This change from a regionally focused command in JSOTF-TS facilitated the needed adjustments in the Mali engagement strategy.

This Mali focused special operations command element soon realized, from the previous engagements and assessments, that the ETIA was not the engagement partner they needed to be paired with. The Malian military did not have a unit that had the capabilities needed to combat the growing influence of AQIM in the north, so the SOFLE sought to create one. The only unit that could provide the personnel and initial equipment to establish a counter terrorism force was the 33rd *Regiment des Commandos Parachutistes*.[90] Within the *Regiment des Commandos Parachutistes*, a new unit known as the *Company Forces Speciales* (CFS) was created. Though named as a company, the CFS became the reaction battalion for northern Mali. The adjustment to the engagement campaign was planned to make the CFS fully mission capable in five years, by 2015. Through enduring engagement, the special operations efforts created a CFS selection course, core of NCOs, and began facilitating the unit's equipping. The CFS expansion was cut short, but the spread of instability spurred by the Libyan regime change in 2011-2012. Tested in combat in the north, the CFS was able to conduct multiple missions where they used combined arms maneuver and inflicted damage on the AQIM groups they engaged with.[91] Unlike the CFS, the majority of ETIA units in the north disintegrated under the Tuareg separatist/AQIM offensive and left most of their weapons and equipment for the enemy.

---

[89] Powelson, 33.

[90] Ibid., 34.

[91] Ibid., 50-54.

Key Takeaways from Mali

At the beginning of the involvement of US SOF with the Mali military, there were issues establishing and transitioning between Special Operations Command Europe and USSOCAF. Following that transition of authority, the creation of the SOFLE and JPAT in Mali gave USSOCAF the tailored command structure needed to make adjustments to the special operations engagement campaign strategy in Mali. The significant changes were the creation of a new Malian special operations unit (CFS) and shifting from episodic to enduring engagement. The combination of the establishment of a tailored TSOC forward command focus, shift to enduring engagement, and the selection of the right engagement partner present the key considerations demonstrated by SOCAF in Mali.

Philippines

Following over a decade of engagement with the Armed Forces of the Philippines (AFP), the JSOTF-P will dissolve their command by the end of 2014.[92] This does not mark a loss of relations between the US and Filipino governments or militaries, but the evolution of a successful SSR partnership. The US military, primarily SOF, will continue military engagement with the AFP to assist in fighting terrorism and delivering humanitarian assistance throughout the Philippines. Key to the engagement strategy of JSOTF-P was the whole of government SSR coordination with the country team and interagency partners, an indirect operational approach, and an enduring special operations command. Through this study, the JSOTF-P and USSOCPAC approach will be analyzed to present considerations and models to avoid and employ during planning and execution of special operations engagement campaigns.

---

[92] Sneha Shankar, "US to dissolve anti-terror group, JSOTF-P, in Philippines after 10 years of fighting Abu Sayyaf," *International Business Times,* June 26, 2012, accessed July 13, 2014, http://www.ibtimes.com/us-dissolve-anti-terror-group-jsotf-p-philippines-after-10-years-fighting-abu-sayyaf-1612340.

Threat

Understanding the context of Filipino threats requires a brief analysis of the operational environment. An archipelago of over 7,000 islands situated 500 miles off the southeastern coast of Asia, the Republic of Philippines has been a strategic hub in the Pacific Ocean for the United States for over a century.[93] The major islands from north to south are Luzon, Samar, and Mindanao. The capital of Manila is a port city in Manila Bay, on the northern island of Luzon. The Filipino population is comprised of a mix of Asian populations and settlers from neighboring Indonesia and Malaysia.[94] This created a blend of more than a hundred ethnic tribes, speaking seventy different languages that are still constantly disputing on Filipino national interests and leadership. Following the United States defeat of the Spanish Navy off Luzon Island, the Philippines were ceded to the United States in the 1898 Treaty of Paris.[95] The United States was met by a Filipino rebellion from the start of the occupation, thus starting the Philippine-American War.[96] After the capture of the guerilla leader Emilio Aguinaldo, a peace was established in 1902 between the United States and the Philippines, except with the Islamic Moros on the southern island of Mindanao.[97] This separation of differences between the Filipinos on Luzon Island and Islamic Moros during the peace of 1902, will continue to be exhibited throughout Filipino history. During the time of decolonialization, the 1934 Tydings-Mcduffie Act provided a pathway to become a fully independent nation by 1946.[98] After the people of the Philippines approved a

---

[93] Center For Army Lessons Learned (CALL), "OEF Philippines," *CALL Newsletter* 10, no. 5 (November 2009): 9.

[94] Ibid., 12.

[95] Department of State, "Background Note: Philippines," January 31, 2014, accessed August 10, 2014, http://www.state.gov/r/pa/ei/bgn/2794.htm.

[96] CALL, 9.

[97] Ibid.

constitution, the Commonwealth of the Philippines was established in 1935.[99] This pathway to independence was interrupted by the Japanese occupation in 1941, forcing the government into exile until the US reinvasion from October 1944-February 1945.[100] The Philippines achieved full independence on July 4, 1946.[101]

Since their independence, the Philippines have constantly been challenged by having a government that is inclusive of all the disparate populations throughout the island chain. This has led to the creation of separatist groups. The two primary separatist groups are the Moro National Liberation Front (MNLF) and the Moro Islamic Liberation Front (MILF).[102] The strategic goals of each of these separatist movements are the creation of Islamic autonomous areas in southern Philippines, mainly Mindanao and Sulu Islands. The primary religion in the Philippines is Christianity, comprising about ninety-five percent of the population.[103] The remaining five percent are Muslim, but make up about twenty percent of the southern population on Mindanao and Sulu Islands.[104] The Muslims in these areas assert territorial claims that date back to the Spanish colonial reign in the Philippines.[105] The MNLF was created in 1971, following clashes

---

[98] CALL, 9.

[99] Ibid.

[100] Ibid.

[101] Ibid.

[102] Benedicto R. Bacani, Special Report 131, *The Mindanao Peace Talks: Another Opportunity to Resolve the Moro Conflict in the Philippines* (Washington, DC: Institute for Peace, January 2005), accessed October 15, 2014, http://www.usip.org/sites/default/files/sr131.pdf, 2-3.

[103] Ibid., 3.

[104] Ibid.

[105] Ibid., 4.

between Christians and Muslims in Mindanao.[106] The armed wing of the MNLF, once totaling 30,000 soldiers, trained in Malaysia and then conducted guerilla operations in Mindanao.[107] Different ideals on how to combat the AFP operations against the MNLF in the early 1980s led to fracturing between the moderate and conservative factions of the group. This fracturing created the MILF in 1981, with the conservative ideals of continuing a violent insurgency.[108] In the early 1990s, the MNLF began peace talks with the Filipino government. These talks concluded in 1996, with the agreement to create the Autonomous Region in Muslim Mindanao (ARMM).[109] The ARMM met the strategic goal of the MNLF, but left more to be desired from the MILF.

The MILF wanted more autonomy than was given in the ARMM, specifically a MILF led governance structure for the region. The armed resistance of the MILF continued after the ARMM was established and was further strengthened by the merging of efforts with Jemaah Islamiyah (JI) in 1999.[110] Formed in 1971 by Abu Baker Bashir, the strategic goal of this Islamic extremist group is to create an Islamic State that contains the territories of Indonesia, Malaysia, southern Philippines, southern Thailand, and Singapore.[111] They also have ties to another splinter group of MNLF, Abu Sayyaf Group (ASG). Like MILF, ASG split from the MNLF in the early 1990s, to seek more conservative violent approaches against the AFP and southern Filipino population.[112] Meaning "bearer of the sword" in Arabic, ASG is an Islamic extremist group that

---

[106] CALL, 16-17.

[107] Ibid.

[108] Bacani, 4.

[109] Ibid., 2.

[110] CALL, 6.

[111] Ibid., 5,14.

[112] Ibid., 15.

has the strategic goal to create a separate Muslim state for the Philippines Muslim population, not just an autonomous region.[113] ASG and JI both have close ties with Al-Qaeda core leadership, having leadership and soldiers who fought with the Mujahedeen during the Soviet occupation of Afghanistan. Though no longer having reported ties to MNLF, these Islamic extremist groups retain the ability to recruit and move relatively uninhibited amongst the Muslim population in the ARMM. Peace talks began with the MILF in 2005, concluding with the signing of a four-part agreement to establish an autonomous region, to be called Bangsamoro.[114] Once ratified by the Filipino congress, a Bangsamoro Transitional Authority will be established by the Moro population, until fully autonomous by 2016.[115] The Bangsamoro agreement and Bangsamoro Transitional Authority will replace the ARMM that was established with the MNLF, further creating friction between the disparate Muslim groups. Even with these advancements in peace talks, the conglomeration of Islamic extremists and active separatist groups in Mindanao and the southern Philippines continues to be the primary threat to stability in the southern Philippines and surrounding Pacific region.

The last major threat against the Filipino government is the Communist People's Party. Originally comprised of tenant farmers of Luzon Island, the Communist People's Party gained popularity in the pursuit of agrarian land reform in the 1960s.[116] This led to the creation of the Communist People's Party military wing known as the New People's Army (NPA).[117] At their height in the 1980s, the NPA had 25,000 guerilla fighters, but through Filipino government

---

[113] CALL, 15.

[114] "A Peace Agreement in Mindanao: A Fragile Peace," *The Economist* 410, no. 8872 (February 1-7, 2014): 33-34.

[115] Ibid., 34.

[116] CALL, 13.

[117] Ibid.

33

reform and AFP targeting, the group has been greatly reduced.[118] Unlike the MNLF and MILF, the NPA operate primarily in the rural areas of Luzon Island and have cells in Manila. The NPA also poses a threat to US personnel in the Philippines assisting the Filipino government or AFP. The distillation of the grievances and strategic goals of all these separatist, Islamic extremist, and communist comes down to the control and distribution of land in the Philippines.

Ends, Ways, and Means

With the primary threats to Filipino stability being the continued guerilla operations from separatist (MNLF and MILF) and Al-Qaeda affiliates (JI and ASG) in the southern Philippines; the ends (objectives), ways (how), and means (resources) that special operations engagement applied to these threats will be analyzed. Like in Mali, as the global counterterrorism campaign synchronizer for the DOD, a primary objective for USSOCOM is to combat the spread and influence of JI and ASG in the Pacific region. Within the Philippines, these efforts indirectly target the operational strongholds in Mindanao and Basilan Islands, the Sulu Archipelago. Seen as a constraint by some special operations leaders, US unilateral offensive operations in the Philippines are prohibited by the Philippine constitution. This constraint creates the opportunity for the special operation engagement strategy to focus on FID with the Philippine Security Forces to support SSR. As a conduit to pursue this objective against JI and ASG, the FID efforts are aimed at building cooperation between the Filipino government and Moro populations and sustaining a Philippine Security Forces opposition to instability in southern Philippines.

The ways in which special operations has engaged with the Philippines has changed over time. Prior to 9/11 the 1st Special Force Group (Airborne) was conducting FID with AFP elements on an enduring basis. Though continuous, this engagement was not implemented under a special operations campaign plan from USSOCPAC. After a change of power within the

---

[118] CALL, 18.

Filipino government and the inclusion of Operation Enduring Freedom-Philippines to the combat ASG, Pacific Combatant Command, USSOCPAC, and the US Embassy country team in the Philippines designed a truly "whole of government" approach to the Filipino sources of instability.[119] This approach is completely banned through the Filipino government and AFP. Initially, this operational approach was direct and concentrated on targeting of ASG through counterterrorism operations.

Following the kidnapping of US tourists by ASG in June 2001, USSOCPAC deployed special operations trainers to create a national counterterrorism capability within the AFP.[120] Like in Mali, the special operations trainers pulled soldiers and talent from existing units within the AFP. The Light Reaction Force (LRC) was formed from the ranks of the AFP special forces and ranger units.[121] From the unit's inception, the special operations advisors recognized that the Light Reaction Force lacked the national command and control to employ the force in combat operations.[122] After completing the initial training, the LRC were deployed to Basilan Island to address the ASG hostage problem.[123] They employed the LRC as conventional forces on Basilan, and not as the counter-terrorism unit they were trained and designed for. This misemployment led to the request from USSOCPAC for additional SOF advisors and command to train, advise, and assist the LRC. The initial USSOCPAC command unit deployed to the Philippines was Joint Task

---

[119] Richard Swain, *Case Study: Operation Enduring Freedom Philippines* (Washington, DC: United States Army Counterinsurgency Center, American University, October 2010), accessed October 15, 2014, http://www.worldcat.org/title/case-study-operation-enduring-freedom-philippines/oclc/716158427?referer=di&ht=edition, 2.

[120] David S. Maxwell, "Operation Enduring Freedom – Philippines: What Would Sun Tzu Say?" *Military Review* 84, no. 3 (May/June 2004): 20. Colonel Maxwell commanded JSOTF-P (2006-2007).

[121] Ibid., 21.

[122] Ibid.

[123] Ibid.

Force 510 (JTF 510)[124] Deploying under the guise of conducting an exercise, named Balikatan (meaning "shoulder-to-shoulder" in Filipino), JTF 510 advised the AFP on a "clear, hold, and build" counterinsurgency and counterterrorism strategy on Basilan Island.[125] The AFP counterterrorism operations combined with civil-military operations during Balikatan resulted in the United States and Filipinos "building 81 kilometers of road, improving and airfield and port facility, and digging fresh water wells" on Basilan Island.[126] This limited direct counterterrorism approach by JTF 510 against ASG on Basilan Island was expanded to include the entire Sulu Archipelago and Mindanao. This expanded area of operations led to the replacement of JTF 510 by JSTOF-P in September 2002.[127]

This original JSOTF-P, up to January 2009, mission read, "In coordination with the U.S. country team, is to conduct FID with the AFP to defeat ASG and JI high value targets (HVTs), and neutralize enemy safe havens."[128] The desired end or objectives for JSOTF-P are that the leadership and safe havens of ASG and JI are neutralized and conditions for them to operate in southern Philippines are not present anymore.[129] The operational approach was expanded to be more of an indirect strategy across the entire joint area of operations, with priority areas being Jolo Island and Central Mindanao. This was different from the direct approach used by JTF 510 on Basilan Island. To execute this operational approach JSTOF-P employed four lines of effort. They are "capacity building, targeted CMO, information gathering and sharing, and information

---

[124] CALL, 18.

[125] Maxwell, 21.

[126] CALL, 18.

[127] US Special Operations Command-Pacific (USSOCPAC), "Special Operations Command-Pacific," accessed August 23, 2014, http://socpac.socom.mil.

[128] CALL, 1.

[129] Ibid.

operations/influence operations."[130] To enable the needed country team, interagency, and national AFP HQs coordination, the Manila control element was established.[131] The Manila control element ensured the JIIM unity of effort needed across all the JSOTF-P lines of effort. This unity of effort included a partnered effort between special operations Civil Affairs teams and existing USAID programs. The synching and de-confliction of efforts and strategies led to a better execution of the targeted civil-military operations line of effort.

Complicating the JSOTF-P mission is the restriction against SOF supporting the AFP in targeting or operations against the MILF or NPA insurgents. This restriction turned out to be another opportunity to JSOTF-P, as it used the targeted civil-military operations and information/influence operations lines of effort to degrade the influence, freedom of movement, and support of the MILF and NPA in the southern Philippine Muslim populations. The indirect approach on these separatist and communist groups has addressed the systemic problem the Filipino government has historically had with the Muslim Moro population. This had led to more acceptances within the Moro population of the AFP operating in the southern Philippines to target ASG and JI and facilitated the recent peace talks between the Filipino government and MILF. With over a decade of implementing the JSOTF-P campaign plan, the combined effort of the United States and Philippines has defeated the majority of ASG and JI threat by addressing the root causes of instability in the Moro populations. As of August 2014, the current JSOTF-P mission is "at the request of the Philippine government, JSTOF-P works together with the AFP to fight terrorism and deliver humanitarian assistance to the people of Mindanao."[132] This change of

---

[130] Major Stuart L. Farris, "Joint Special Operations Task Force-Philippines," (monograph, School of Advanced Military Studies, U.S. Army Command and General Staff College, Fort Leavenworth, KS, May 2013), 34.

[131] CALL, 3.

[132] USSOCPAC, "US Special Operations Command-Pacific."

mission displays three key points. The first is the sustained acknowledgement of the sovereignty of the Filipino government. The second is the indirect approach through the delivery of humanitarian assistance. The final key point is that JSOTF-P, and future USSOCPAC forward commands, continues the enduring SSR commitment and relationship to combat insurgency and terrorism within the Pacific region.

Key Takeaways from the Philippines

Throughout the US engagement with the Philippines since 9/11, USSOCPAC constantly assesses and tailors the special operations engagement strategy to meet the SSR need outlined by the US country team in Manila. Key to the engagement strategy of JSOTF-P was the whole of government SSR coordination with the US country team and interagency partners, an indirect operational approach, and an enduring special operations command. The DOS, DOD, and USAID combining, and not duplicating efforts demonstrated a balanced SSR approach. The engagement strategy was built around a SOF campaign, with a lasting commitment to reach the desired mission in the Philippines. In keeping with the SSR tenant of focusing on the population, the indirect operational approach conducted was not only able to combat the external terrorist threats, but also provide a pathway to solve long standing internal issues between the Filipino government and ethnic Moro population. As the operational environment changes in the Philippines, USSOCPAC continues to tailor the needed engagement and special operations command to meet the SSR needs of this key Pacific ally.

Considerations for Special Operations Engagement

During this research, understanding of different special operation engagement campaign approaches to support DOD's efforts in SSR, is analyzed through two recent case studies. In each case, there are good practices and lessons revealed as the different TSOC's strategy is executed. The following considerations are not only supported by the analysis of the case studies, but also reinforced theoretically by deterrence theory, organizational theory, and the emerging theory of the prevention of war through special operations engagement. From these practices and lessons, there are five key considerations for future special operations engagement. First is the need for enduring engagement with partner forces. Second is the establishment of long-term special operations engagement campaigns by the TSOCs that are flexible enough to adapt to changing operational environments. Though it might seem obvious in SSR, the third consideration is the unity of effort between DOS, DOD, and USAID. Next is the establishment of a tailored TSOC forward command to support the engagement strategy. The final consideration is the need for the selection or creation of the right partner, with the right capabilities, and in the right location to support the SSR objectives. The grouping of these considerations provides TSOCs with a model to adjust or construct special operation engagement campaigns or strategies that support the DOD's effort in SSR.

Enduring Engagement

The SOF Operating Concept and *SOCOM 2020* are built on the tenant of enduring engagement for the future development of special operations. In Mali, the shift from episodic to enduring special operations engagement began developing the desired HN capacity and capabilities needed to combat the country's threats to stability. From the beginning of Operation Enduring Freedom-Philippines, the special operations effort was built on enduring engagement with the AFP, resulting in completing the initial JSOTF-P mission and more internal stability in the Philippines. In establishing the GSN, an increase in enduring engagement during TSCP operations will be vital to forming and keeping those HN partner relationships. The primary constraint to enduring engagement is the limited amount of SOF available to conduct operations. To plan with this constraint, the engagement with each country in a TSOC's AOR must be prioritized and engagement events tailored to support the host country's needs. This will mitigate a common approach of episodic engagement every few years or with different HN partners, which are counterproductive to building any enduring HN capacity or capabilities. The consideration of enduring engagement directly supports the next consideration of establishing long-term special operations engagement campaigns.

Special Operation Engagement Campaigns

The central ideal of special operations engagement is that "you can't surge trust."[133] To prevent wars in the future, the United States cannot expect to begin to develop the needed trust with HNs as combat operations commence. That demonstrates the need for not only enduring engagement with partner forces, but also the planning of and execution of special operations campaign. Understanding that by joint doctrine campaigns are planned and executed by GCCs or JTFs, these engagement campaigns would support the TCP, TSCP, and country IDAD. These campaigns would ensure that SOF providers would continue to advance partner capacity and capabilities, and prevent a constant retraining of basic skills if it is not needed. The TSOC is the command where the engagement campaigns should be planned and managed because of the operational control relationship with the GCCs, access to country teams through forward special operation commands, and link to special operation force providers. As this multifaceted conduit, the TSOC can adjust the engagement campaign to meet the evolving needs of the GCC or country team, while ensuring that the special operation force provider is executing the correct operation to support these changes. In leveraging the transformation of TSOCs highlighted in *SOCOM 2020*, more assets can be allocated within the TSOC to conduct the campaign planning, management, and liaison to strengthen these engagement efforts.

---

[133] USSOCOM, *Special Operations Forces Operating Concept*, 6.

Unity of Effort

The concept of SSR is built around the unity of effort between the DOS, DOD, and USAID. All too often though, the SSR coordination does not prevent the disparate approaches from being executed and duplication of efforts. This issue is evident in the Mali case study, as the DOD engagement effort was focused on the source of instability in northern Mali, but was sparingly supported by the DOS and USAID efforts. This de-coupling of approaches provides more risk to the aim of preventing war or conflict in the country or region. Conversely, the unity of effort demonstrated in the Philippines provides the desired whole of government approach to align US political and military objectives and connect DOS and USAID programs to the HN through the special operations engagement. Though most of this SSR coordination is conducted at the embassy or consulate, the engagement consideration of a tailored TSOC forward command can improve this coordination and prevent actions that increase HN instability.

Theater Special Operations Command Forward Commands

There are many options to establishing a TSOC forward command. This variance ranges from a two to three manned special operations command forward (SOCFWD) at the embassy to a special operation battalion augmented JSOTF. In each of the researched cases, the use of different command structures are shown. The tailoring of these commands to support the special operations engagement is significant to achieving the desired SSR objectives. The use of a regional JSOTF, like JSOTF-TS, can synchronize the special operations effort across multiple countries, but increases the risk of not having the needed SOCFWD to each country. This risk is shown in the early stages of Mali, which led to the establishment of the SOFLE and JPAT by USSOCAF. Another consideration for SOCFWD establishment, is the use of a separate special operations liaison element at the embassy to support a larger SOCFWD or JSOTF that is not located near the embassy or consulate. This was done by JSOTF-P through the establishment of Manila control element to better the unity of effort and coordination between the command and country team.

41

Also, as the special operation engagement campaign changes in scope, the SOCFWD needs to be adjusted to meet the increased or decreased special operations demands in the country. This adjustment was conducted in each case, as the special operations engagement in Mali was halted due to the coup and the replacement of JSOTF-P with a smaller SOCFWD due to a change of mission. This flexibly in TSOC forward commands provides the SSR actors and special operation force providers with the needed enduring commands to support the engagement campaigns and strategies for the host countries.

Host Nation Partner Selection

The final, but one of the most critical engagement considerations is the selection of the right partner, with the right capabilities, and in the right location for SOF to engage with. These three separate elements for the right partner selection need to be meet to support a progressive engagement campaign. The right partner for SOF usually consists of the counterterrorism, infantry, and host country national mission units. Engaging with other partners, like armored or artillery units, can be outside the scope of SOF FID training and is more suited to partnering with US conventional military units. A partner in the right location was important in each of the researched case studies, allowing for targeted special operations engagements in the needed area of the host country. Another important consideration for the right partner and capabilities, is if the partner's missions and threat focus align with the US interests in the country or region. If the right partner cannot be identified to engage with, negotiations can be conducted with the HN and country team to create the right partner. This was conducted in Mali and the Philippines, as new units were formed from and within existing HN units. The advantage to this approach is that partner forces are formed from the ground up and can be augmented by DOS military procurement. The risk is that it can take years to make the units fully mission capable, as was the case of the CFS in Mali. This risk exposes security HN vulnerabilities to threats to stability in the country or region.

Recommendations

Through the analysis of the case studies and identifying the command considerations to future special operations engagement, there are three recommendations to enable increased support to the DOD's effort in SSR. First is to create or bolster systems within the TSOCs to implement the special operation campaign development and management. There are opportunities to do this through the TSOC initiatives outlined in *SOCOM 2020*. Second is through the addition of liaisons at the special operation force provider's planning cells, these TSOC systems can connect the force provider to the TSOC forward command and update to the engagement campaign. This connection will enable the force provider with the needed information to facilitate planning and execution of engagement operations, that progress partner force's capacity and capability within the engagement campaign's initiatives. The final recommendation is more proactive partner selection for engagement operations. Identified previously as a key consideration, partner selection cannot simply be left up to the request of the HN or random selection by the country team. Negotiations should be conducted between the TSOC forward command, HN, and country team to ensure that the right partner is selected to support the engagement campaign plan. The combination of these recommendations and considerations will provide the needed special operation support to DOD's effort in SSR, to prevent future wars

Bibliography

Bacani, Benedicto R. Special Report 131, *The Mindanao Peace Talks: Another Opportunity to Resolve the Moro Conflict in the Philippines.* Washington, DC: Institute for Peace, January 2005. Accessed October 15, 2014. http://www.usip.org/sites/default/files/sr131.pdf.

Bennett, John T. "Pentagon: All U.S. Elite Commandos in Mali 'Accounted for'." *U.S. News,* March 23, 2013. Accessed June 17, 2014. www.usnews.com/news/blogs/dotmil/2012/03/23/pentagon-all-us-elite-commandos-in-mali-accounted-for.

Berkowitz, Bruce. "Proliferation, Deterrence, and the Likelihood of Nuclear War." *The Journal of Conflict Resolution* 29, no. 1 (1985): 112-136.

Blumenfeld, Max R. "Training in Trans-Sahara Africa." US Africa Command, December 13, 2010. Accessed July 12, 2014. www.africom.mil/Newsroom/Article/7896/training-in-trans-sahara-africa.

Brodie, Bernard. "The Anatomy of Deterrence." *World Politics* 11, no. 2 (January 1959): 173-191.

Center for Army Lessons Learned. "OEF Philippines." *CALL Newsletter* 10, no. 5 (November 2009): 9-12.

Central Intelligence Agency. "Mali." *The World Fact Book,* June 20, 2014. Accessed June 25, 2014. www.cia.gov/library/publications/the-world-factbook/geos/m1.html.

Department of Defense. *National Defense Strategy.* Washington, DC: US Government Printing Office, June 2008.

_____. *Quadrennial Defense Review.* Washington, DC: US Government Priniting Office, March 2014.

_____. *Theater Campaign Planners' Handbook.* Washington, DC: US Government Printing Office, February 2012.

Dorrie, Peter. "U.S. Special Operations Forces Screwed Up in Mali: Why Years of Military Cooperation Achieved So Little." The Medium, April 23, 2012. Accessed June 17, 2014. www.medium.com/war-is-boring/u-s-special-operations-forces-screwed-up-in-mali-643bc779751c.

Douglas-Bowers, Devon. "The Crisis in Mali: A Historical Perspective on the Tuareg People." Global Research, February 1, 2013. Accessed June 27, 2014. www.globalresearch.ca/the-crisis-in-mali-a-historical-perspective-on-the-tuareg-people/5321407.

Farris, Major Stuart L. "Joint Special Operations Task Force - Philippines." Monograph, School of Advanced Military Studies, U.S. Army Command and General Staff College, Fort Leavenworth, KS, May 2013.

Fowler, Robert. *A Season in Hell: My 130 Days in the Sahara with Al Qaeda.* Toronto: Harper Collins Publishers, 2011.

Gresham, John D. "SOCOM: Finding Certainty in Uncertain Times." *The Year in Special Operations, 2014-2015 Edition* (June 2014): 18-29.

Headquarters, Department of the Army. Army Doctrine Reference Publication 3-05, *Special Operations.* Washington, DC: US Government Printing Office, August 2012.

Joint Cheifs of Staff. Chairman of the Joint Chiefs of Staff Manual 3113.01A, *Theater Engagement Planning.* Washington, DC: US Government Printing Office, May 2000.

_____. Joint Publication 3-0, *Joint Operations.* Washington, DC: US Government Printing Office, August 2011.

_____. Joint Publication 3-05, *Special Operations.* Washington, DC: US Government Printing Office, July 2014.

_____. Joint Publication 3-22, *Foreign Internal Defense.* Washington, DC: US Government Printing Office, July 2010.

_____. Joint Publication 5-0, *Joint Operation Planning.* Washington, DC: US Government Printing Office, August 2011.

_____. Joint Publication Note 1-13, *Security Force Assistance.* Washington, DC: US Government Printing Office, April 2013.

Joint Special Operations Task Force-Trans Sahara. "Mission." US Special Operations Command-Africa. Accessed July 12, 2014. www.socafrica.mil/component/ JSOTF-TS.asp.

Joint Special Operations University. *Special Operations Forces Reference Manual, Third Edition.* MacDill Air Force Base, FL: Joint Special Operations University Press, 2011.

Kegley, Charles, and Shannon Blanton. *World Politics: Trend and Transformation.* Boston: Wadsworth, 2012.

Kuhn, Thomas S. *The Structure of Scientific Revolutions.* Chicago: University of Chicago Press, 1970.

Livingston, Thomas K. Congressional Research Service Report for Congress R41817, *Building the Capacity of Partner States Through Security Force Assistance.* Federation of American Scientists, May 2011. Accessed October 15, 2014. http://fas.org/sgp/crs/natsec/R41817.pdf.

Maxwell, David S. "Operation Enduring Freedom - Philippines: What Would Sun Tzu Say?" *Military Review* 84, no. 3 (May/June 2004): 20.

Odierno, Raymond T., James F. Amos, and William H. McRaven. White Paper, *Strategic Landpower: Winning the Class of Wills.* The Official Homepage of the US Army Training and Doctrine Command, October 2013. Accessed October 15, 2014. http://www.tradoc.army.mil/FrontPageContent/Docs/Strategic%20Landpower%20White%20Paper.pdf.

Ogilvie-White, Tanya. "Is There a Theory of Nuclear Proliferation? An Analysis of the Contemporary Debate." *The Nonproliferation Review* (Fall 1996): 43-60.

"A Peace Agreement in Mindanao: A Fragile Peace." *The Economist* 410, no. 8872 (February 1-7, 2014): 33-34.

Petit, Brian S. "Breaking Through the Tension: The Operational Art of Special Operations in Phase Zero." Monograph, School of Advanced Military Studies, U.S. Army Command and General Staff College, Fort Leavenworth, KS, May 2013.

_____. *Going Big by Getting Small.* Denver, CO: Outskirts Press, 2013.

Powelson, Simon J. "Enduring Engagement Yes, Episodic Engagement No: Lessons For SOF From Mali." Masters thesis, Naval Postgraduate School, Monterey, CA, 2013.

Sagan, Scott D. "The Perils of Proliferation: Organization Theory, Deterrence Theory, and the Spread of Nuclear Weapons." *International Security* 18, no. 4 (Spring 1994): 66-107.

Seely, Jennifer C. "A Political Analysis of Decentralization: Coopting the Tuareg Threat in Mali." *The Journal of Modern African Studies* 39, no. 4 (2001): 499-524.

Shankar, Sneha. "US to dissolve anti-terror group, JSOTF-P, in Philippines after 10 years of fighting Abu Sayyaf." *International Buisness Times,* June 26, 2012. Accessed July 13, 2014. www.ibtimes.com/us-dissolve-anti-terror-group-jsotf-p-philippines-after-10-years-fighting-abu-sayyaf-1612340.

Swain, Richard. *Case Study: Operation Enduring Freedom Philippines.* Washington, DC: United States Army Counterinsurgency Center, American University, October 2010. Accessed October 15, 2014. http://www.worldcat.org/title/case-

study-operation-enduring-freedom-philippines/oclc/716158427?referer=
di&ht=edition.

Turabian, Kate L. *A Manual for Writers of Research Papers, Theses, and Dissertations,
Eighth Edition: Chicago Style for Sutdents and Researchers (Chicago Guides to
Writing, Editing and Publishing).* Edited by Wayne C. Booth, Gregory C.
Colomb, Joseph M. Williams and the University of Chicago Press Staff. Chicago:
University of Chicago Press, 2013.

US Department of State. "Background Note: Philippines," January 31, 2014. Accessed
August 10, 2014. www.state.gov/r/pa/ci/bgn/2794.htm.

_____. "Security Sector Reform," February 2009. Accessed February 25, 2014.
www.state.gov/documents/organization/115810.pdf.

US President. National Security Presidential Directive-44, "Management of Interagency
Efforts Concerning Reconstruction and Stabilization." Washington, DC: The
White House, December 7, 2005. Accessed October 15, 2014. http://www.irisc.
net/site/Library/nspd-44.pdf.

US President. *National Security Strategy.* Washington, DC: The White House, May 2010.
Accessed October 15, 2014. http://www.whitehouse.gov/sites/default/files/
rss_viewer/national_security_strategy.pdf

US Special Operations Command. *SOCOM 2020.* Tampa, FL: US Special Operations
Command, May 2013. Accessed October 15, 2014. http://www.defenseinnovation
marketplace.mil/resources/SOCOM2020Strategy.pdf.

_____. *Special Operations Forces Operating Concept.* Tampa, FL: US Special
Operations Command, May 2013. Accessed October 15, 2014.
http://fortunascorner.files.wordpress.com/2013/05/final-low-res-sof-operating-
concept-may-2013.pdf.

US Special Operations Command-Pacific. "Special Operations Command-Pacific."
Accessed August 23, 2014. socpac.socom.mil.

Wulf, Herbert. *Security Sector Reform in Developing and Transitional Countries.*
Research Center for Constructive Conflict Management, Germany, 2004.
Accessed October 15, 2014. http://wulf-herbert.de/Berghofdialogue2.pdf.